just breathe

eleven mantras + tools for heart healing

maia thom

for everyone out there
who is showing up for themselves
to heal + do the work

i see you

"why eleven?"

my mother asked me this question when I told her of my idea to create this short collection of the mantras, thoughts + practices I've been sitting with recently.

there are many sacred numbers, to be sure. three is a sacred number – we look at the ancient religions, the trinities imbued in our lives and cultures, natural and manmade alike, and we see just how important it is. seven is a sacred number, a number of renewal, ritual, holiness and relationships. nine is a lucky number, a number of good fortune – it indicates change is coming and it will benefit all of humanity; it is tolerant of others, and it is wise.

so why eleven?

I surprised myself with the answer. I shrugged, "eleven is the number of Friendship." my mother was surprised, she hadn't heard this before. I went on to explain how in astrology, the eleventh sign of the zodiac, Aquarius, is the sign that rules the individual within the collective while the eleventh house rules friendship. this energy is eccentric and forward-thinking, here to lead us into the future in a new way that will benefit all. it is curious and stubborn but also extremely intelligent; and best of all, eleven is not here to fit in. it is here to embody all of itself and show us how to do so in the process.

regardless of whether or not you believe in astrology, my intention in creating this book was just that: friendship. connection. I wanted to make something that would remind people that they're not alone in the messiness of life – that we're all just figuring it out, and it's so much more fun if we are able figure it out together.

in the midst of the chaos of 2020, here is a space for you to reconnect with your heart and begin embodying all that you are.

in these pages, you'll find a series of mantras + tools that I've been using to build a strong foundation within myself, ones I come back to time and time again. I hope they spark something in you. this is also an invitation for you to begin building your own toolbox – what works for one person may not work for everyone, and that is okay. but you are so much more capable than you think. you can do this.

I can't wait to see all you will become.

in friendship and love,
maia xx

the world needs you to be you.
let's begin.

one
all of me

i allow myself
to be seen
for all of
who i am.

just breathe | maia thom

something I've been sitting with a lot recently is my secret desire to be seen.

at some point when I was a child, I picked up the patterning that this desire was selfish. that was the last thing I wanted to be, so I grew to block myself from being seen in a big way.

whenever I would start to succeed, old habits would come in to sabotage me, self-doubt would take over as I believed I wasn't worthy of love, of support, of being seen. the things I had to say weren't valuable, because I was too young.

whenever someone would offer me a compliment, I would respond, "really? you really think I'm good at this?" or I would find some way to deflect it.

sometimes I think we run away from the things we're good at because it makes us uncomfortable. we take for granted that which comes easily to us – it feels so natural, like breathing, so we decide therefore it must be less valuable. we were taught value only what comes through struggle and hard work, or we simply compare ourselves to other people, seeing them fill the spaces where we feel inadequate and longing to be as good as they are at what they do.

the beliefs surrounding this patterning are vast and complex: maybe we fear being seen because it was dangerous when we were young; hiding became a defense mechanism to keep us safe in the midst of trauma. maybe we learned that we were supposed to fit in, because if we didn't none of the other kids would like us – I know I lived that one. maybe we were told we weren't worthy of success because of circumstances outside of our control, or because the adults in our life were carrying so much of their own trauma, allowing us to show up in our brilliance would have been too painful to watch.

there are a million reasons that can keep us small, but the first thing to know is that awareness is the first step.

the world needs you to show up in your brilliance, as you are.

just breathe | maia thom

what would happen if you didn't fail?
what would happen if you received everything you've always wanted?

sometimes we fear our success even more than we fear our failure because
success means change. stepping into our light may put us in situations
unfamiliar and unknown. but the opposite, to remain in our smallness, is an
incredibly unsatisfying way to live.

when you show up in your light, you show others it's possible to do the
same.

what could you become if you allowed yourself to step into all you're meant
to be?
get curious of your brilliant light + follow where it leads.

exercise:
write down 11 things you appreciate in others – these can be qualities,
skills, accomplishments etc. now ask yourself (or someone you trust) which
of these do you already embody? often when we see things in others, it's
because they already exist within ourselves. see yourself as you are, truly.

two
cyclical nature

i trust the
cyclical nature
of my process.
i am healing+
i am whole
as i am.

sometimes it's hard to be patient with the process.

I'm not sure when it happened but at some point, in my teenage years,
I picked up the belief that it's not okay to stop, sit still, or rest for any
prolonged period of time. if you stop, you might never start again. sitting
still made you lazy. life is short, you must fill every moment of your time or
else you're wasting it.

~~we live in a society, too, where this way of life is the norm. every year
around the beginning of January, we set goals and plan our lives and seek to
learn how we can be more 'productive' with our time, as if time is finite and
we never have enough of it.~~

the problem with this mentality is that eventually, you burn out. this
happened to me just before I turned twenty, after a particularly rough
four months filled with several curveballs. my body said NO MORE and
demanded that I rest. so, somewhat begrudgingly, I did. as I did, as I've
spent more and more time with myself in the past two years, life has
reminded me of something beautiful: *I've always had a deep love for sitting still.*
I'd just forgotten.

when I was a child, I had no problem spending hours 'doing nothing.'
on long car rides, I would sit and look out the window, just watching the
landscape and enjoying the worlds in my head. I liked to sing a lot and play
pretend. with such an active imagination, I was hardly ever bored – and I
was an only child, so most of the time there was no one else to entertain me.
I was quite comfortable being alone.

as I grew older, I inherited this guilt around time spent not 'being
productive.' it became increasingly uncomfortable for me to sit still for long
stretches of time, and I measured the value in my days by how much I got
done. I have a bit of an excessive streak and so I took this to the extreme, yet
I didn't see a problem with how I was living. I was too deeply entrenched in
the doing to see how unhappy I had become.

I am writing these words in 2020, and so if you are reading this it means you
will know what I mean when I speak of the Great Pause. in the first half of
this year, the world quite literally stopped. I'd never experienced anything
like it, I don't think any of us have, really. the streets were so quiet, and

everything was unknown, still is unknown as to how the repercussions of this time will unfold.

I live alone in a small apartment in a city several thousand miles away from my family, and so this span of uninterrupted time has allowed me to get to know myself on a deeper level, to sit in my own vibration and become intimately familiar with my heart + mind. as I've done so, I've begun to find my own rhythm for how I like to go through life.

when there is nowhere to go and no one to distract you, you start to get clear on a lot of things. things you like, things you don't like, where your strengths + weaknesses lay, and what it is you really want. I started a meditation and contemplation practice every morning, and the ritual has changed my life.

meditation, or *listening to silence* as I like to think of it, is much simpler than we think. it's not about being perfect, it's just about creating space. space to observe and witness what is going on, so we can see our thoughts + emotions as opposed to simply embodying them.

as I became more aware of my thoughts, I've become more aware of a lot of things.

the thing I've noticed the most is how everything ebbs + flows. my emotions: there are days where I'm feeling high on life, and other days where I feel quite low. my creativity: some days I'm all ideas, some days I'm hands on creating, and other days my mind is much more analytical and better suited to mundane tasks. my energy: some days I am full of it and other days I just need to rest.

the more I've leaned into this natural ebb + flow, the more I grow, and the easier life becomes, too.

when we resist our fatigue, we tend to be much less productive than if we were to rest and come back at it tomorrow. same thing goes for it we're feeling restless – maybe that's the time to go for a walk and move your body as opposed to sit down and force yourself to focus. maybe once you've moved your body, it will be a lot easier to sit down and get to work.

just breathe | maia thom

the thing is to learn to *trust* that you'll circle back around to the things that
need to get done. the more we are able to live in sync with our internal
rhythm, the more efficient we become.

this can occur in small ways as much as it can in big ones. maybe you can't
take a day off right now, but you can lay on the floor for five minutes and
not look at your phone. (I do this all the time, it's one of my favourite ways
to regenerate energy.) maybe you're feeling agitated by that comment your
co-worker made on your last email, so you put on a song and dance around
behind closed doors for three minutes to *shake it out*.

nature flows in cycles, and we do too.
nothing to be ashamed of.

exercise:
take a few moments throughout the day to check in with yourself – where is
your energy at, how are you feeling emotionally, what does your body want
to be doing, what is your mind telling you? you can set reminders on your
phone. if you do this for a span of 30 days, you'll start to get a feel for when
you get tired and when you're energetic, when you're happy and when
you're low. see if you can start making tiny adjustments accordingly.

three
support

i allow
myself to receive
support.

receiving. giving. these two things are intricately linked.

I think many of us – especially sensitive or empathic people – develop a comfort around giving, often stepping into roles of being the nurturer, the rescuer, the helper, or simply the one known for taking care of others. we are led to believe it's selfish to receive, and we shove our desires to the side, putting everyone else's needs above our own.

but your ability to receive is intricately linked to your ability to give. as we've all heard so often, you can't pour from an empty cup. you have to fill yourself up and allow yourself to receive if you want to continue to give and provide from a generous, wholesome place.

sometimes it's a pride thing. we develop an identity around being the giver, and we wonder who we are if we're not giving all the time. we wonder where our value is. sometimes it comes from a place of lack of trust – trust that others can take care of themselves, trust that those who are giving to us come from a pure intention. sometimes it comes from a lack of self-worth. we believe we are not worthy of receiving good things, that we needed to have done something to deserve it.

by refusing to receive, we're actually not doing anyone any favours. if everyone is giving all the time, there is no one to receive. eventually, givers become burnt out and the giving no longer comes from an easy place – when this happens, it becomes strained for everyone involved, even if no one has the language to voice it.

and so, we are led back to the concept of *balance*.

one of my close friends likes to refer frequently to the equation of alchemy. giving and receiving must be in balance or in time, the exchange becomes instable and ultimately implodes. it's not about going through life in a way that is transactional, but rather simply being aware. and asking for what you need.

sometimes, too, we think the answers to our problems lay in working harder.

just breathe | maia thom

we forget we have a relationship to life as well, that the universe does not just put us here and abandon us but wants to help us along our path. we often block ourselves from receiving without even knowing it, believing things need to be hard. lacking trust, we focus on all the ways things have gone wrong in the past and ask why it would ever be any different in the future.

another platitude: where attention goes, energy flows.

if you look for problems, you're going to find more problems. if you look for solutions, chances are, you're going to start finding solutions.

what would it feel like to be abundant in joy? in support? in energy? in love? sit in that vibration for a moment. allow yourself the space to dream that it's available to you – just open up to the possibility, even if you don't believe it yet. because it is. all those good things are available to you if you're willing to let them in.

exercise:
soften + allow. we choose what kind of energy we allow into our space – what are you saying yes to right now? what do you need more of? make a short list of these things, and then instead of focusing on how much they are lacking, get curious. manifestation can be playful! in fact, it's often more fun and effective if it is.

to really sit in this vibration, you can do a simple meditation. if sitting in silence feels too daunting, put on some soothing music (Spotify and YouTube have many options) and find a place to get comfortable for a few minutes. as you close your eyes, tune into your body and become aware of the breath, simply watching the rhythms that come up. once you've settled, make sure your head is up, chin level with the floor, spine comfortably aligned. then, begin to image yourself surrounded by a soft light in the colour of your choosing. I like pink, but green or yellow can also be nice. like pillows, clouds or cotton candy, this energy is sitting all around you, supporting you in whatever way you need. stay for as long as you like.

let yourself be held; you are safe here – you are loved.

four
thoughts on thinking

just because you think it
doesn't make it true.
just because you think it
doesn't make it true.
just because you think it
doesn't make it true.

I ask myself this question a lot these days. I think it is quite easy to default to panic in a world that seems to be falling apart faster than we can pick up the pieces. life is a lot right now, that fact in undeniable.

but also. sometimes *all* it takes is a simple question, a simple moment of grounding in the present moment to realize you are not in imminent danger.

just because you think it, doesn't make it true. just because you think it, that doesn't mean it's going to happen. just because things seem difficult doesn't mean we won't make it through.

when we encounter a harsh image or nasty thought, we get to choose what we do with it. do we acknowledge it, transform it, take appropriate action and shine a light into the darkness? or do we sit in fear, paralyzed by our mistrust in life + its 'inability' to take care of us? (we are not victims here.) your experience is valid. but we can always choose how we show up.

show up with love.

exercise:
sit with whatever energy it is you are feeling and begin to identify where it sits in your body. is it anxiety, fear, doubt, shame or anger? oftentimes these things congregate in the chest, making it hard to breathe, or they live in the belly and give us a stomach-ache.

first ask: is this mine? sometimes we receive information from people we come in contact with throughout our days and find ourselves shouldering energy that isn't ours to carry.

if it is yours, ask: is this current or is this from the past? sometimes we feel a very intense emotion come up, but it's really just an old pattern playing out until we become aware of it.

then, verbally give yourself permission to release it. the best way I've found to do this is through *movement or conscious emotional release.*

this looks like:
put on some loud music in a safe space, plant your feet hip width apart, keep your arms loose at your sides and start bouncing lightly from your knees, allowing the motion to shake your whole body. you can also shake out your hands, and if you feel called to do so, open your mouth and let out whatever sound feels the need to come out, or sing along to the music. after a few minutes, this shaking becomes automatic. shake for at least ten minutes. when you finish, you may like to lie on your back on the floor. if you feel a little buzzy, this is normal.

you can also do a conscious emotional release by going somewhere safe, like your bedroom, closing the door and quite literally acting out your anger. throw a tantrum on your bed, punch a pillow or jump on your mattress and scream (into your pillow if you're worried about the neighbours.) make sure you don't have anything breakable nearby! and take care of your body also.

both of these practices can lead to tears, the third emotional release I've found to be very effective. when you're going to have a good cry, it's important make sure you feel safe. I like to sit with my knees hugged into my chest, usually on the floor with my back against the wall. sometimes in order to get the tears flowing, I will quite literally say to myself, "it is safe for you to cry" or "you're allowed to cry." here's a friendly reminder that tears do not make you weak! we all have moments we just need to let it out, however ugly it may appear on the outside.

when you finish your emotional release, you may like to journal about the experience. or find some funny dog memes, because who doesn't need more of those in their life?

I know this is hard work, but you're brave and I honour you for doing it.

five
renewal

Whenever we grow, there is a shedding of the old to make room for the new. A renewal, of sorts.

some days, growth will leave you feeling raw, exposed + deeply vulnerable.
I think it's important to know that this is perfectly normal – there's nothing
wrong with you.

letting go is hard. as humans, we can be a bit of a walking contradiction.
some of us are wired to hold onto things, because change feels scary. others
have a tendency to flit from one thing to the next, never going deeper than
the surface because that kind of depth or intimacy requires commitment,
which feels frightening. on some level, I think most of us have both these
energies inside of us: the one that likes movement and the one that likes to
be still. we just tend to have one we favour over the other, and the one we
avoid, we avoid for a reason. it makes us uncomfortable.

truthfully, we need both. our brains crave novelty – when we stop learning,
we lose something. we grow stagnant. but if we choose to engage with life
and get curious about the things we don't know, we can continue to expand
our minds all our lives.

in order to make space for the new, we must let go of the old.

I've been doing this a lot recently. the process can be deeply uncomfortable
at times – when you start to release connections to people, places, or
identities you've become attached to, it can quite literally feel like a part of
you is dying.

a friend of mine has grown fond of the analogy of the butterfly. before
the caterpillar can grow beautiful wings and fly away, it wraps itself in
a cocoon and melts in order to develop into its new form. sounds pretty
uncomfortable to me. also. sounds pretty accurate.

so if you're in the midst of a period of growth or spiritual awakening right
now, know that it's okay to feel a little more fragile than you normally
would. you are going through a lot, shedding old beliefs and ways of being.
like that caterpillar in the cocoon, when you emerge, you'll carry with you a
newfound wisdom + freedom to go wherever it is you've been dreaming of.
but for now, it's okay to feel like a mess. you're not alone.

please be gentle with yourself; you are a work of art.

just breathe | maia thom

exercise:
make space for self-care – this evening, curl up with a blanket and a good book or movie, something that inspires your curiosity. maybe watch some videos or interviews with someone you admire. permission to be soft or whatever you need in this moment.

six
growing through
discomfort

i acknowledge that what
i am doing is new, there
is uncertainty here +
that may trigger my
doubts, insecurities or
fears. i choose to stand
in courage + build my
life one step at a time,
in the direction i desire.

just breathe | maia thom

just start.

you have an idea of something you want to create or explore, and you're
really excited about it. you feel like you're standing on the precipice of
something big (or something small) but either way it gets your heart
pumping a little quicker or brings a smile to your face. the only problem is,
you don't know how to go about getting started.

it feels daunting and unknowable, this big thing. so maybe, you think, I'll
just wait a little longer. or you talk yourself out of doing the thing altogether,
because really, what is the point? why take a risk when you're comfortable
where you are?

I've tried a lot of things in my life – and I've 'failed' a lot, too. my brain
comes up with ideas pretty constantly, and just by nature of the way I am
wired, I like to bring these ideas to life in the real world, or at least attempt
to do so.

when I was 10, I started my first business with a friend, Heart Balloon Ink.
she made jewelry and I sewed things, mainly pillows with pockets on the
front, or what I liked to call 'pillows with a purpose.' the business didn't last
long, but it was good fun while it did, and the intention was there. about 11
years later, as I step into my own creative entrepreneurial endeavors, I can
see how everything I've tried up until this point has led me to where I am
today.

I never would have acquired all this knowledge if I'd been too afraid to take
the first step and *just start.*

I could tell you many more stories of things I've tried and 'failed' at, like the
many writing contests I entered and didn't win or the novel I tried writing
at age 16 that I never finished, but the point is this: if you never take the first
step, you'll never know where something will lead. sometimes it's not about
finishing the thing, either. sometimes you'll start a project and you'll realize
it's not for you – in which case, you can change course and try something
different.

sometimes it is about finishing the thing, even if it makes you
uncomfortable.

just breathe | maia thom

here's a gentle reminder that you don't need to know the whole path before you take the first step, and failure is part of the process. just take it one step at a time.

you've got this.

exercise:
that thing you've been dreaming about for a while? let's find a way to get started.

first: write down the big goal or vision you have for what it will look like in the end. fill in as much detail as you like, really let yourself dream and write freely, without letting judgment or logic get in the way of what you think is possible. this is really just to get the creative juices flowing, our vision usually evolves once we start taking action anyways.

second: identify why it is you want to do this thing. does the idea of it bring you joy? do you want to help people? is there something you want to share or become through the process? this step is important – your purpose can be simple, but it's helpful to have one. when the going gets tough (as it sometimes will) you can come back to why you began, and it can motivate you to keep going. so don't skip this one.

third: let's break it down. what are the steps required to accomplish this thing? what can you do on a monthly, weekly, or daily basis to start moving towards what you want? you can have a few different layers of action, but try to make the steps as small as possible. this will help it to feel less daunting.

for example, say you want to learn how to play 'stairway to heaven' on the guitar because music brings you joy and you've always loved listening to guitar, so it's something you want to learn. you could commit to playing guitar for five or ten minutes every day before dinner. (attaching the new habit to something you do every day makes you more likely to follow through on it.) you say you're going to learn five new chords this month. then you'll learn a basic song. find some tutorials on YouTube. and so on and so on …

fourth: take the first step!
fifth: keep doing it!

optional: tell a friend what you're doing and have then keep you accountable. some of us function better when other people are involved, and if this is you, lean into it!

extra credit: do a little research! choose three people whose life story or work you admire and do a little digging on the internet to find out more. how did they get to where they are today? where were they when they started? what were the messy bits of their story? learning about people we look up to can help us feel a little less alone in our own journey, help us to have patience with the process, and inspire us to keep going when things get tough. you're not alone ;)

seven
desire

i am becoming
intimately familiar
with my heart's
deepest desires.

desire. what a funny word.

it varies greatly depending on the culture you grow up in, but this is one of those words that exists within a vortex of conflicting opinions. when we're pulled in so many different directions at once, it can be hard to decipher where we stand within ourselves. especially if you have the slightest inkling to be a people pleaser.

sometimes I think we become so caught up in what everyone else wants for our lives that we forget to check in with what it is we *truly* desire, deep inside. knowing this, like so many other things, requires silence and stillness to hear. silence and stillness can be uncomfortable. we don't always like what comes up.

too often, we judge ourselves for our desires – maybe they're 'too simple' or maybe they're 'too much to ask.' maybe we feel like we're the only ones that want the things we do, and so out of fear of what others may think of us if they found out, we pretend our desires don't exist. we feign interest in other things and live the life we're *supposed to* live as opposed to the one we want to.

but the only way to live a life that is truly your own is to get acquainted with that inner voice and *listen.* truly. what pulls at your soul? what lights you up?

what do you want to do with this one precious life?

desire doesn't always feel like a fiery, burning passion. sometimes it shows up as curiosity – something catches your eye and draws you in, or you feel a pull to do things differently. find small ways to encourage + follow those notions when they come up.

living in this way doesn't mean you have to leave the life you've built all at once; it's much more incremental. you could start a hobby on the side during weekends or make a plan to go on vacation somewhere you've always wanted to go. you could read new books or watch a tv series on something that intrigues you, try a new recipe or take a class that seems completely unrelated to everything you've done up until this point.

just breathe | maia thom

invite this more playful energy into your days + watch your life change in subtle ways that bring you more joy.

life is more fun when you're exploring.

exercise:
now, I may be a little biased seeing as I am a writer, but I find journaling to be an incredibly useful tool to get acquainted with your inner voice. if you don't like writing things out by hand, you can record yourself speaking into the voice recorder on your phone. the point is to get your thoughts out of your head into a form where you can take some space from them and see them more clearly.

in *stream of consciousness journaling,* we ask ourselves a question and then just pour out whatever comes. proper grammar and eloquence of speech do not matter, no one will read (or listen to) this except for you. once you've chosen your topic, you set a timer and go for ten minutes nonstop – when the pen hits the paper or you begin to speak, don't judge or censor what comes up, just let it flow. if you still have more to say once the timer goes off, you can keep going. having a time frame when you start this exercise just helps it to feel less daunting.

when you've finished with the exercise, take a break before you read or listen to it. you can even wait a full day if you like, to really gain perspective.

some questions to explore:
what do you need more of right now?
what are you missing in your life?
what is one thing you miss doing from childhood?
what was your favorite thing to do as a child, the thing you didn't want to stop doing?
what is one thing you would do, if you knew you could not fail?
what is one time perfectionism held you back from doing something you wanted to do?
if you could travel anywhere in the world, where would you go?
what would it look like for you to prioritize your well-being?
how would you like to feel in your friendships?
how would you like to feel in love?
what brings you joy?

just breathe | maia thom

eight
why not me?

When good things
do come, instead
of asking,
"Why me?"
try asking
"Why not me?"

worthiness. do you believe you are worthy of a beautiful life?

sometimes in life, we develop a resistance to receiving good things. it often happens when we've lived through a few challenging moments, where we got sidetracked by a painful curveball we never saw coming or we failed at something we were wholeheartedly committed to. after those few occurrences, some part of our brain can adapt to live on high alert, always searching for the next disaster.

we almost expect things not to work out in our favour. in a way, this is a defense mechanism: it's more painful to get your hopes up and have them dashed than it is never to get your hopes up in the first place. also, we tend to like to be right, and anytime we put ourselves out there, there is an element of the unknown. we don't know how it's all going to work out, and we don't always like that.

but this 'expecting bad things to happen' doesn't have the affect we hope it to. instead of saving us from failure and rejection, it almost makes those things more likely to happen. we subconsciously block ourselves from the success we've grown to believe is not possible, and we lose confidence in ourselves.

yes, there is such a thing as barking up the wrong tree, or not knowing when to pivot in a new direction when things clearly aren't working out – but I also see how so often we drive ourselves too far in the opposite direction, killing our dreams before we even have a chance to take the first step.

when good things *do* happen, as they will, we question them. we see all the times things didn't work out and we blame ourselves, thinking this time will be no different.

what if it could be different? what if things don't have to be so difficult all the time?

this is a lesson I've been learning in my life recently: when you're following the flow of the things that are meant for you, *it doesn't have to be hard.* sure, there will be times when you encounter challenges, but it shouldn't feel like a constant uphill battle. process over results – are you enjoying the day to day of what it is you are set out to achieve? if not, it may be worth taking a deeper look at why you've set your eyes on this goal in the first place.

sometimes we watch someone we respect receive success, recognition, or fulfillment in a way that we crave for ourselves, and so we decide if we want that thing, we must follow in their footsteps and set out on the exact same path they took to get there.

what we fail to recognize is that each person is wired differently and exists within a unique set of circumstances, so what works for one person will not necessarily produce the same results for another. one of my favourite quotes goes something like this: 'if you can see the whole path laid out in front of you before you take the first step, it's probably not your path.'

when I was young, I was convinced I wanted to go to the Olympics for artistic gymnastics. I watched Nastia Liukin flip and twist her way to the gold medal at the Beijing Games in 2008, and I decided that one day, I would be standing on that podium just like her. I spent the next eight years pursing this goal relentlessly, pushing my body and mind to the max and beating myself up each time my efforts fell short of my own high standards. I suffered several injuries and an eating disorder and lived in a heightened state of anxiety most of the time.

still, it wasn't enough.

at sixteen, I reached a career high followed by a personal all-time low. the day I was supposed to go back to the gym after my week-long Christmas break, I cried for two hours before my coach convinced me to show up for practice. a little more than a month later, I ended up fully tearing an important ligament in my knee that forced me to reconsider my next course of action.

I chose to leave artistic gymnastics for circus, something else I'd been training in all my life. at the time, it was liberating – I believed the circus world allowed space for my creativity in ways the rules of gymnastics would not. again, I set my eyes on someone else's path and pursued it with rigor. again, life redirected me in a series of somewhat painful events.

and that leads me to where I am today. it's been two years since I finished my time at the national circus school, and I've found my way to a life I truly love. now I'm in the process of learning how to believe I truly deserve it.

I recently discovered my own discomfort with receiving good things, and that is why I wrote this short reminder. sometimes we just have to reframe the question. when good things come, instead of asking, 'why me?' try asking, 'why not me?' and see what happens.

exercise:
remember that life is magic. the most beautiful things can happen when we let go of our need to control every single step of the process and decide to co-create with the universe instead. that being said, work is still required. one thing you can do is start rewiring the subconscious beliefs that may be blocking you from receiving the support and love you deserve.

one way I like to do this is through written affirmations. there is a secret here, though. it's not about repeating the same phrase over and over a million times until you zone out and the words are drilled into your head. our minds actually retain information better when there is variation in our repetition, so I like to *write out ten to fifteen different mantras* instead of writing out the same mantra ten to fifteen times.

this is most effective if you do it regularly, at least a few days per week. if you're having a moment of self-doubt, instead of reaching for something to numb out, grab your notebook and affirm the qualities you want more of in your life.

I am enough
I love my body, my body is a sacred space
I am supported, I am held, I am loved, I am safe
my feelings are valid
my hopes, dreams and desires are valid
I speak my truth with kindness
I welcome good things with an open heart
I have everything I need
I allow myself space to rest + heal
I hold space for my highest expansion
I lovingly set boundaries
I allow myself to be seen
I am worthy of success, love (insert desire here)
I allow myself to receive support
I allow my creativity to flow freely
I trust my intuition
I trust abundance comes to me with ease
I take aligned action towards my desires
I am open to receive opportunities that are aligned with my joy + purpose
I release all that which is not mine to carry
I can empathize with people's pain without needing to live it for them
I choose to align myself with the energy of well-being

nine
messy bits

i am learning
to hold my own
hand through the
messy bits +
remember how
supported i am.

just breathe | maia thom

life is *messy.*

we like to pretend it's not, but it is. none of us have it all figured out all of the time. even the people you think have it all figured out – maybe they're in a good moment in their lives, or they're just really good at acting. the truth is that they too, have gone through a lot to get to where they are, and they will undoubtably go through the mess again one day in the future, to get where they're going.

this is all coming from a recovering perfectionist – for a lot of my life, I've done my best to avoid showing the messy bits to give the impression that I've had it all together.

as a child, I embodied this to the extreme. I hardly ever fell or scraped my knees playing outside. I hated getting dirty – the first time I went to the beach, I refused to take off my shoes because I didn't want to get sand stuck all over my feet. I thought it would feel yucky. and when I was learning to read, I would practice reading those picture books aloud several times to make sure I got it right: once to myself, once to my father to make sure I wasn't making any mistakes, and only *then* would I read it to my mother when she came home from teaching at the end of the night.

this idea of perfectionism can hold us back from doing a lot of things and create stress where there doesn't need to be any. somewhere along the line, I took on the identity of being this perfect little girl who never did anything bad or got into trouble. everyone expected it of me, so I expected it of myself, too. in time, it grew to manifest itself in every aspect of my life.

when I was fourteen, it showed up as an eating disorder. when I was sixteen, it manifested itself as intense self-loathing + fear in my gymnastics training. when I was nineteen, it showed itself in my first relationship where I was so scared of messing things up, I never voiced my standards or spoke up about the things that made me uncomfortable.

perfectionism creates unnecessary pressure. we build these standards for ourselves that we can never live up to and yet still, we feel like failures when we don't 'succeed.'

I didn't always used to be this way. before the age of five, my mother could hardly get me to tidy up my bedroom no matter how hard she tried. it looked like a tornado had touched down most of the time – there were things strewn about the floor, a real lack of order, yet I was blissfully happy and unaware.

then I turned five or six, and something happened. it was like a flip switched on, and I became a completely different child. I can't even remember what exactly happened to make me shift my tune so drastically, I just recall how one day, the order and cleanliness I'd avoided became utterly important. everything had a place and that was where it lived, and my room was a mess no longer.

the one area of my life where I've never really felt the pressure to be perfect has been my writing. it's a constant process of evolution for me, and the most natural part of my being. I'm sure there have been moments where I've experienced writers block, usually when there were some strict parameters involved and I felt boxed in by what I was supposed to create. inevitably, I would step away from the writing to do something else and when I came back, words were already flowing freely. they popped into my head when I was in the shower or walking down the street, and now it was my turn to get them down on paper and flow with what came.

for some reason, I've always had this different approach when it came to writing – I knew it required a lot of practice, a lot of submitting to publications where I would probably be rejected and yet, I felt I had nothing to lose by trying, so I did. I knew I would keep writing regardless of what happened, and I knew if I kept showing up, the writing would grow as I did. I trusted the process.

recently, I've been starting to apply this approach to life on a grander scale, letting go of my old need to be *perfect*. part of the magic of being human is in the messy bits, the parts where life doesn't go according to plan yet somehow, you end up exactly where you need to be in time.

no one has it all figured it out. we're all in the process of living this thing called life, and life is messy. it does become a lot less lonely when you're willing to share the mess with others; they remind you that you're not alone and, as spiritual leader Ram Dass always said, *we're all just walking each other home.*

just breathe | maia thom

part of the journey of learning to embrace the messy bits is making a commitment to no longer abandon yourself.

take a moment to sit with yourself and reconnect with your body, your breath. if it helps, you can close your eyes, or allow your gaze to soften and turn inwards, to the rhythm of your own heart.

now use this simple mantra: *I welcome my energy home to myself.* it is a gentle calling, not a scrambling or desperate energy but simply an invitation to wholeness. repeat the words many times for as long as you need, and imagine your light rejoining your being. this is enough. this is all you need.

ten
mutlifaceted

there is no one
'right way' to do
things, no one
'right way' to live
this beautiful life.
don't let anyone
tell you otherwise.

just breathe | maia thom

multifaceted.

we are multifaceted human beings. I find I have to remind myself of this so often as my mind wants to simplify things, make everything back or white. I am this *or* that. I can't be strong + sensitive or serious + funny. I can't be smart + creative + athletic all at once.

but why can't I be?

there is this funny dual expectation in our society: we 'must' be good at all things, yet we 'can't' be good at many things at once so we 'have to' choose.

but who wrote those rules?
maybe it's time we get curious and write our own.

exercise:
sometimes we inherit stories from society and the people around us about who we should or should not be, what is 'ideal,' and what is possible versus what will 'never happen.' everyone is and should be allowed to have their own opinion, but that doesn't mean it has to be yours. it's important to ask ourselves where our beliefs + stories have come from, otherwise we may live based off a script that's outdated or belongs to someone else.

this exercise is simple. take an area of your life where you feel limited or strained – for example, look at your relationship with money. what stories did your parents have around money growing up? what phrases did they repeat over and over again? was there the belief that 'money doesn't grow on trees?' were they meticulous savers, or did they spend freely and end up in the stress of debt? now look at your own beliefs surrounding this area. what phrases do you find yourself repeating? what stories do you believe? question them.

this same approach can be applied any time we come upon a limiting belief. perhaps you believe no one will ever love you, or that you're too much work – why? we need to take accountability for our actions, but we also need to ask ourselves honestly where we've fallen into patterns because it's familiar and we feel safe.

you can work your way through the different areas of your life: family, relationships, friendship, career, balance of giving and receiving, physical and mental health.

where did this story come from? and what story could I be telling instead?

another powerful tool here is the *questions we ask ourselves.* I love this idea from Jim Kwik, a memory expert who speaks about the importance of the thoughts we allow to walk through our minds.

in his work, Kwik shares the concept of *dominant questions:* what is the question you ask yourself most often in a day? keep track + observe over the course of a week, and it will tell you a lot about your subconscious patterning.

for example, if you are constantly asking, 'how can I get people to like me?' your brain will look for the answers, and you will live from a place of reacting to the needs of those around you as opposed to living your own life. on the contrary, Kwik found in conversation with Will Smith that the dominant question the renowned actor asks himself is 'how can I add magic to this moment?' this mindset is proactive as opposed to being reactive + still seeks to serve.

the questions we ask ourselves are deeply powerful. take a look at yours.

eleven
when doubt surfaces

just like everything else, our courage flos in waves. it's natural, when you are in the midst of trying new things, to find yourself at the low tide of self doubt.

you are so brave♡
just for taking the
steps you are taking.
when the doubt
surfaces, remember
why you began +
breathe through it.

ultimately, we are humxn.

we can be doing all the right things – reflecting, meditating, exercising, eating + sleeping well, succeeding in our professional life and fulfilled in our relationships at home – and still, self-doubt surfaces. this is natural, it's part of the process. you're not going to be feeling confident all the time, especially if you're trying new things.

it's important to remember progress over perfection, in our internal world as much as our external one. it's not about never getting triggered, never tripping up or doubting your abilities, it's about how you *respond* when those things do happen.

it's not about being perfect.

let me say that again: it's not about being perfect. we are spiritual beings having a humxn experience, and so we are going to have humxn feelings + reactions come up from time to time. the more we do the work, the more space we are able to create to witness the parts of ourselves we're not necessarily proud of in order to hold space for their growth + transformation.

when you mess up, how soon can you be ready to apologize? when you come off balance, how quickly do you find your way back to yourself?

it's not about rushing these things, but rather ease of process. non-judgemental way finding. seeing and accepting all of ourselves for who we are, to hold space for our shadow + light + everything in between as we move through the journey of becoming.

all of you is welcome here. all of you is loved.

exercise:
this is a meditation I like to do to reconnect to my essence when I've been pulled away from myself, or simply to ground into my own vibration before stepping out into the world for the day. I invite you to play with the colour of light to see what really resonates for you – it may be blue, purple, green, or any other colour on the spectrum of the rainbow. we each have a unique essence, and you can use this practice to become acquainted with yours.

just breathe | maia thom

begin by settling into a spot where you feel safe + comfortable and you will not be disturbed for a period of time. become aware of the points of contact between yourself and the floor, beneath your seat + your feet, feeling the weight of your body pressing down into the earth. now close your eyes. imagine there is a ball of light living in the base of your belly – it expands + contracts with your every breath, your own personal sun. this is your life force, and it is sacred. take this time to honour it in its light.

stay here for as long as you like. the more often you do it, the easier it will become to sit for longer periods of time. to deeply anchor into this energy, I invite you to do this practice every morning for 21 days. some days will be more interesting than others, but consistency is the key.

be patient, and you'll see just how powerful you truly are.

just breathe | maia thom

All will be
revealed in
good time.

you are in the
sacred space
of becoming.

hi there. you made it! good job.

thank you for coming along on this journey with me. I hope it will be the first of many we walk together. life is so much more interesting with people by your side.

this work is a lifelong process, so please be patient with yourself. the goal is not to do the work all in one shot, but to take it in bite-sized pieces. remember that you are your own best healer; trust what resonates with you and leave the rest.

sometimes healing work is painful, sometimes it's uncomfortable and sometimes, we just don't want to show up at all. it's okay to take breaks from deep diving, come up for air and just be here, just be human. enjoy your physical body. eat some cake. watch a funny movie. have a lighthearted dinner with friends.

healing work isn't about perfection, it's about welcoming more peace into your life in the long term. it's about having those touchstones to return to when life is mind-blowingly beautiful just *as much as* when it's hard. it's about learning what you need to come back on balance, learning what helps you come back to yourself in those moments you stray far away.

just by showing up to read these words, you've already taken the first step. as one of my friends often likes to remind me, once you are aware of something, you can't become un-aware of it. you may not always act on your awareness, and that's okay, too. you're human. just know that even in those moments, your knowing hasn't gone anywhere. the more you practice returning home to yourself, the easier it becomes.

I want you to know that I am so proud of you. you are an incredible human being and, if no one has told you lately, you are so loved. you are so needed. you are here for a reason (as *cliché* as that may sound.)

keep showing up. keep doing the work. and don't forget to celebrate sometimes, too. like today – today is a good day for you to celebrate showing up for yourself. go do something fun.

remember, you've got this.

in friendship and love,
maia xx

maia thomlinson (maia thom) fell in love with words before she could write - from the earliest age, language has been her most constant companion, her way of navigating the world and the thing she could not live without. as a writer and word artist, she works with words to create spaces for people to breathe and come home to themselves. her work is grounding, intuitive, loving and practical, inviting new perspectives into the lives we live and the connection we all share in being human. maia writes the words she needs to hear, and she shares them because she believes if she has experienced something, someone else has, too. you can find her online at **maiathom.com** or on Instagram as **@maia.thom**.

if you want to read more from maia, her first full length collection, *kitchen table talks*, will be avalible in fall of 2020 on Amazon, Chapters Indigo, and many other places books are sold.